ALL in a DROP

How Antony van Leeuwenhoek Discovered an Invisible World

by LORI ALEXANDER

Illustrated by VIVIEN MILDENBERGER

Houghton Mifflin Harcourt

Boston　　New York

To Nelson Alexander, who sees things not only for what they are
but for what they might someday be—L.A.

To my dad, who taught me that the wonders of this world
extend far beyond what the eye can see —V.M.

Special thanks to Douglas Anderson, MFA, professor at Medaille College in Buffalo,
New York, guest researcher at the Huygens Institute for Dutch History in Amsterdam,
and creator of the Lens on Leeuwenhoek website, for reviewing this manuscript and
graciously answering my many questions. Your helpful suggestions and careful attention
to the smallest detail are immensely appreciated. And to my editor, Ann Rider,
who saw potential from the start.—L.A.

hmhbooks.com

The text of this book is set in Bazhanov.
The illustrations in this book were created using pastel, colored pencil and watercolor.
Design by Andrea Miller

Library of Congress Cataloging-in-Publication Data

Names: Alexander, Lori, author. | Mildenberger, Vivien, illustrator.
Title: All in a drop : how Antony van Leeuwenhoek discovered an invisible
world / Lori Alexander ; [illustrator, Vivien Mildenberger].
Description: Boston ; New York : Houghton Mifflin Harcourt, [2018] |
Audience: Ages 7-10. | Audience: Grades 4 to 6.
Identifiers: LCCN 2018051351 (print) | LCCN 2018055849 (ebook) | ISBN
9780358036197 (ebook) | ISBN 9781328884206 (hardcover)
Subjects: LCSH: Leeuwenhoek, Antoni van, 1632-1723--Juvenile literature. |
Microbiologists--Netherlands--Biography--Juvenile literature. |
Biologists--Netherlands--Biography--Juvenile literature. |
Microscopes--History--Juvenile literature. |
Microbiology--History--Juvenile literature.
Classification: LCC QH31.L55 (ebook) | LCC QH31.L55 A44 2018 (print) | DDC
579.092 [B] --dc23
LC record available at https://lccn.loc.gov/2018051351

ISBN 978-1-328-88420-6

Manufactured in USA
PHX 4500795019

Table of Contents

Introduction

Just inside the window, in a bright patch of sunlight, sits a curious man. He lifts an oddly shaped metal bar to his eye. He squints through a tiny hole and doesn't move a muscle. What could he possibly see with a contraption like that?

His name is Antony van Leeuwenhoek (an-TONE-ee van LAY-ven-hook). He has never taken a science class. But he is about to make a discovery that will change the world.

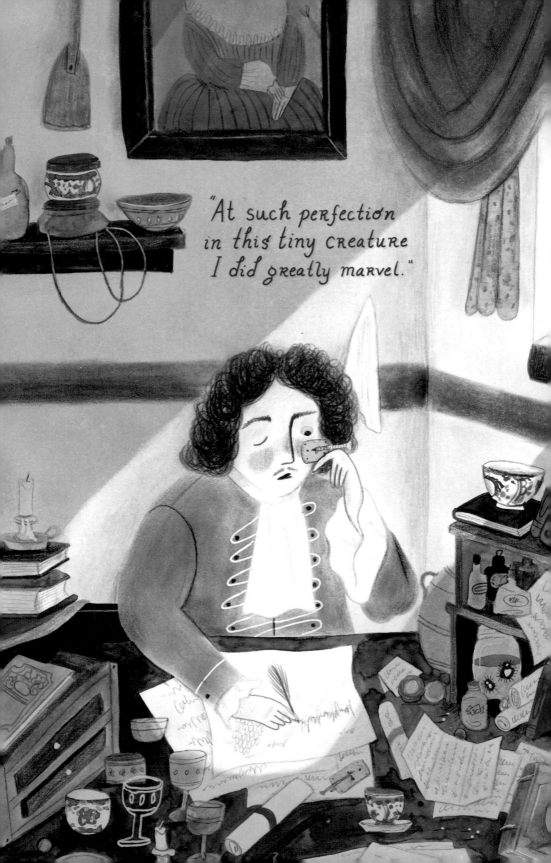

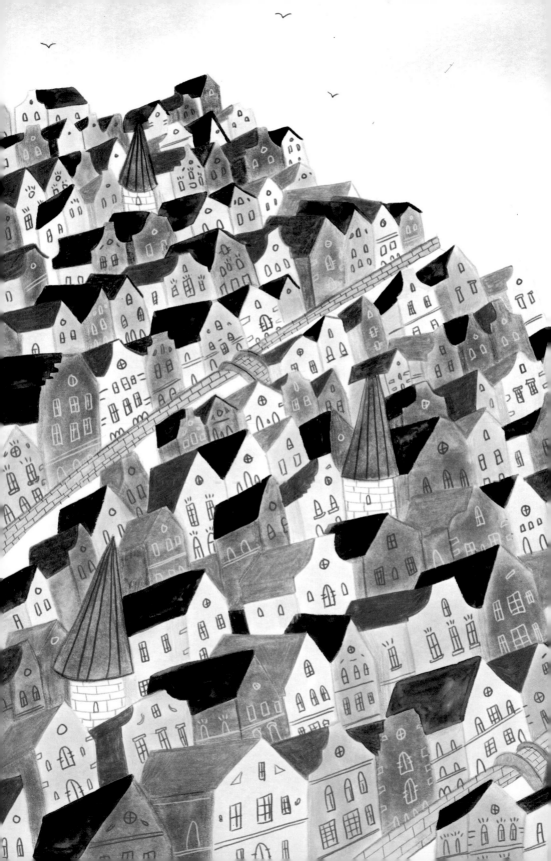

Chapter One:
A Golden Age

In a booming city laced with waterways and bustling with merchants who bellow, *Fresh fish! Furniture! Porcelain tiles! Tapestries!* lives a young boy named Antony.

From the trees that line the canals in his town of Delft, Netherlands, Antony plucks a fistful of leaves. He feeds the tender greens to his pet silkworms. They munch and munch until the leaves disappear. Antony watches closely. Do the silkworms have tiny teeth? He watches one spin a cocoon. Where do those silky threads come from? There is so much his eyes cannot see. But now is not a time for watching and wondering.

His father is calling.

Antony's father is a basket maker. The sturdy wicker baskets he sells are used to pack and protect dishes and other fragile exports that will leave Delft on nearby cargo ships. The large vessels travel both east and west to faraway ports in Africa, India, Japan, the Caribbean islands, and North America. They carry many items for sale and trade: spices, sugar, silks, coffee, tea, silver, ivory. It's the late 1630s, and the Netherlands owns the largest fleet of ships in the entire world. Indeed, it is a profitable time to be a merchant. So profitable, the Dutch (the people of the Netherlands) will later give this period a nickname: the Golden Age.

Antony's mother knows of something golden as

well. Hers is in the form of a crisp, tasty beverage. Her father, Antony's grandfather, was a respected beer brewer. Mugs of ale keep the townspeople happy and healthy. When Delft's water supply is polluted by local industries, everyone, even the children, drinks the low-alcohol beer. Maybe Antony will learn to make bottles of brew and continue the family tradition. One thing is certain: he will learn a trade of some sort, just like his parents.

Antony sells his pet worms to a silk spinner in the market square. Their cocoons will be used to make delicate threads for yarn. The sale earns Antony a small profit. Already, he has a head for business.

Chapter Two:
Big Changes

Antony is still young when his father dies unexpectedly.
Now his mother must care for Antony and his four
sisters all by herself. Before long, she remarries. But her
new husband's home is small and cramped. His mother
has a solution: eight-year-old Antony is sent off to a
boarding school, a place where he will live and study, in
a neighboring city about fifteen miles from Delft.

Antony's schooling is basic. He learns some math.
He learns to read and write in his country's language:
Dutch. He does not study science or learn other
languages, like English or Latin. He doesn't need them.
He is not expected to become a philosopher or a great
thinker. He will grow up to be an ordinary tradesperson,
like his parents.

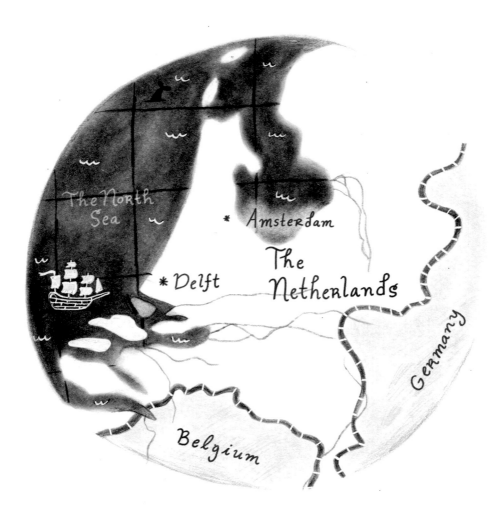

When he is fourteen years old and finished with his
schooling, Antony moves in with his uncle, who is a
lawyer and lives in the city of Benthuizen, about nine
miles from Delft. His uncle makes a promise to Antony's
mother: he will help Antony learn a trade. But Antony
shows little interest in learning about the law and his
uncle's government job. Still, his uncle makes good on
the promise. Antony is sent to Amsterdam for training in
a linen merchant's shop.

Antony is impressed by the city. Amsterdam is
huge! There are 100,000 more people here than
in his hometown. Immigrants come from France,
Spain, and Portugal. In their countries, they were
told which religion to practice. But in the Netherlands
people have more freedoms when it comes to religion
and government. Anyone who works hard is welcome
here. Antony watches the city construction: buildings grow
taller, canals grow wider, houses spring up everywhere.
He visits the bookstores, apothecaries, boot shops,
bakeries, and stores filled with maps and nautical gadgets.
He listens to the traveling musicians. Amid the commotion
of the bustling city, Antony begins his training.

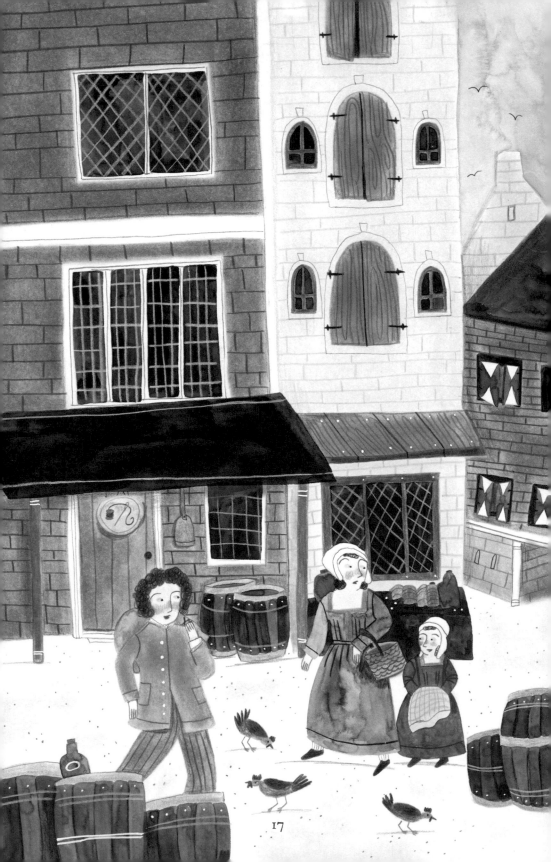

Antony spends the next six years working as an apprentice for a linen merchant. He learns how to assist customers as a sales clerk. He learns how to handle money as a cashier. He learns how to place orders and pay bills. Finally, Antony is ready to open his own shop. By this time, he has had enough of the big-city life. In 1654, at the age of twenty-two, he moves back to Delft. With some money left to him in his grandfather's will and a loan from the seller, Antony buys a house where he will live and set up his shop. He will not weave baskets. He will not brew beer. Antony has mastered the trade of draper.

Growing Up Quickly

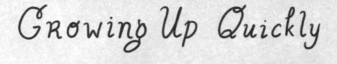

In seventeenth-century Netherlands, and many other places around the world, most children were considered adults by the age of fourteen. Basic schooling might end as soon as their tenth birthday. A boy would typically learn his father's trade or be sent to live with a relative to become an apprentice in the trade of his uncle or cousin. Only the wealthiest families would send their male children to universities to continue their education. Those students would learn Latin and other foreign languages, philosophy, mathematics, physics, astronomy, and other advanced sciences. Graduates would become lawyers, physicians, engineers, or government officials. The education of a girl varied depending on her parents. Some wanted their daughters to have an advanced education including a foreign language. But most girls in the Netherlands received only the basics in spelling, reading, writing, and math (more education than girls received in any other part of the world). After that, they would remain home to learn the housekeeping and child-rearing skills they would need for their likely career of wife and mother, although some women took part in the family business alongside their husband.

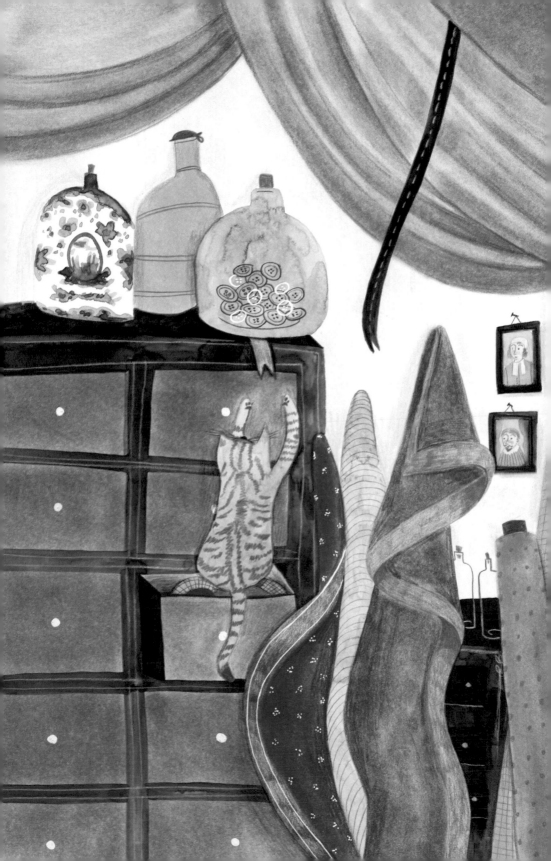

Chapter Three:
Seller of Cloth

A draper is a person who sells cloth. Antony fills
his shop with woven wools, shimmery silks, crisp
taffetas, and bleached linens. People need these
fabrics for all sorts of things: dresses and suits,
pillowcases and sheets, napkins, tablecloths,
window curtains, and furniture upholstery.
Buttons and ribbons fill the shelves as well.

Antony wants to sell quality fabric, so he inspects the cloth closely. Are the fibers straight and strong? He holds up a swatch. His eyesight is good, but he still can't count the tiny threads. How will he know if his fabric is the best? Like other cloth merchants, Antony must use a lens—a piece of glass cut in a special way—to see up close.

He places the circle over the fabric. What does Antony see? Rows and columns of fuzzy fibers. They look more like fat ropes than fine threads.

Verbazend! Amazing!

With his magnifying glass, Antony is able to study his fabric's fibers. He is able to measure thread count—the number of horizontal and vertical threads in a small sample of fabric—to determine the quality of the cloth. The higher the thread count number, the better and softer the fabric. Now Antony can be sure he is selling top-quality cloth.

Focus on Lenses

A **lens*** is a clear piece of curved glass or plastic that bends light. The shape of the lens will determine how the light is bent. There are two basic types of lenses:

A **convex** lens bulges outward—it is fat in the middle and thin around the edges, like a lentil. These types of lenses focus light into a point, like in a magnifying glass.

Convex

A **concave** lens curves inward—it is thin in the middle and fat around the edges, like a bowl. These types of lenses spread light out, like in a flashlight.

Concave

Back in Antony's time, lenses were fairly new. The most common type were lenses placed into metal frames. These became eyeglasses and were used to help people with poor eyesight. In the 1590s, combinations of lenses were placed into metal or wooden tubes to create early telescopes and microscopes. Telescopes helped to view distant objects up close. Microscopes helped to make small objects look larger. Neither tool was very powerful at first, magnifying objects only three to nine times their original size. Lenses would improve over time as more people began to experiment with their form and function.

*The word lens comes from the Latin for "lentil," or lens. This is because a convex lens has the same shape as a single lentil bean.

Chapter Four:
An Eye-Opening Trip

In 1668, at the age of thirty-six, Antony takes a much-needed vacation from his busy shop. He sails to London, England. Perhaps he will visit friends who also sell fabric. Perhaps he will sightsee. In the distance, Antony spots towering, white cliffs. They look as though they're made of chalk. Antony is curious. Once on land, he hikes close enough to scratch away a small sample. When the sample breaks apart, he finds that the bits look transparent, or clear. It's only when the particles are stacked on top of one another that they appear white.

While in London, Antony hears chatter about an English scientist named Robert Hooke, who uses lenses to examine fabric, as well as plants and insects. This scientist uses the lenses in a tool called a microscope. What he sees has been turned into a best-selling book called *Micrographia*. It's the talk of the town!

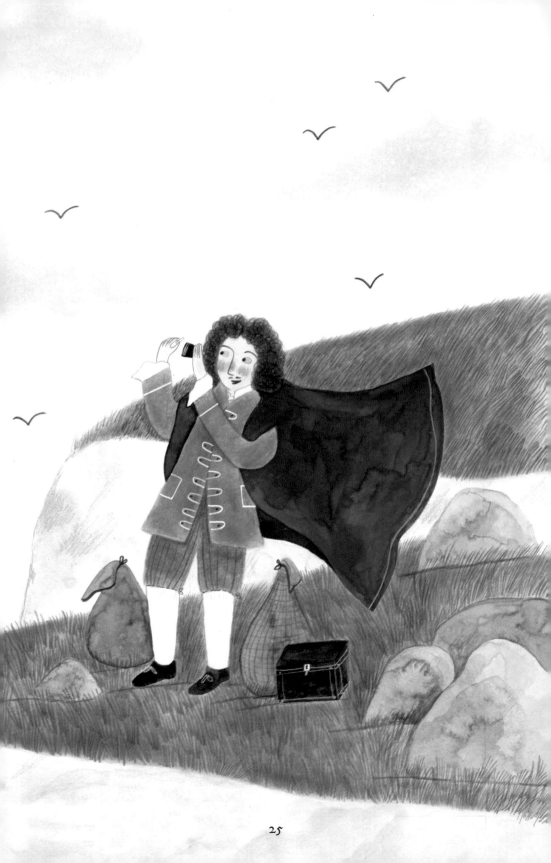

Antony does not know how to read the English words in *Micrographia* because he can only read Dutch, but he is fascinated by the pictures. Some fold out like a map. He sees a flea as big as a cat, a white moth with fine feathery wings, and a louse like a soldier ready for battle. Even ordinary items—the tip of a sewing needle, a piece of cork, a poppy seed—look magical when shown in such detail. Antony is filled with wonder. What other hidden worlds might he find with a microscope like that?

Back home, Antony is determined to build his own kind of microscope. He did not go to school to be a scientist or an inventor. But he is curious. Can he make a microscope more powerful than his magnifying lens?

First, Antony needs a small piece of glass. A bit of broken mirror should do. But the shard is not the shape he needs for his lens. He must grind it to a rounder shape. On the end of a stick, Antony glues the glass.

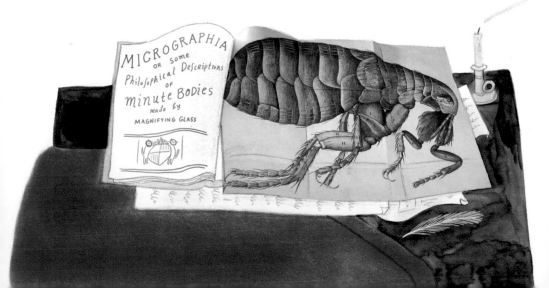

MICROGRAPHIA
OR some
Philoſophical Deſcriptions
OF
minute BODIES
made by
MAGNIFYING GLASS

He uses a mold, a metal plate with a spherical dent,
as his grinding base. A sprinkle of sand goes into the
mold. Antony twists the glass-tipped stick in the mold
until the coarse sand smooths away the shard's rough
edges. He repeats the process with finer and finer sand
on both sides of the glass. His lens is taking shape! But
Antony is not finished. He places a small square of felt
into the mold and a pinch of powdery polish. Again, he
twists and turns the tiny ball of glass. Not too much. He
doesn't want to change the shape, only polish away any
imperfections from the surface of the lens. The process
takes a great deal of trial and error.

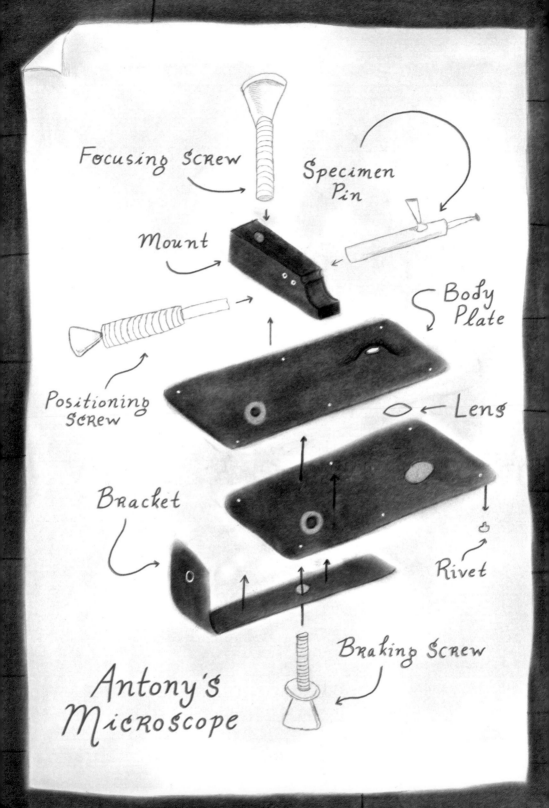

Antony nests the pea-size lens between two small rectangles of brass, each poked with a hole. He seals the brass plates with rivets. Now he must fashion a mount to hold his specimen and a focusing mechanism so the sample will look clear and not blurry. The design takes time. Antony makes his own screws with a foot-powered lathe. Sometimes the screws bend or break. Antony tries again. After several weeks, he has created a system of screws to control the movement of a sharp pin in front of the lens. The pin is ready to hold his first sample—a moldy bit of bread.

Antony throws open the shutters to fill the room with light. He raises the metal contraption to his eye. He turns the screws. The sample moves up and down, side to side, closer and farther. This, too, takes practice. Finally, the sample is in focus. What does Antony see? Tiny mold spores, like the ones Robert Hooke wrote about in *Micrographia*. But surprisingly, the mold looks bigger and even more detailed than the images from the book. Little does Antony know, his hard work has led him to create one of the world's best microscopes.

What will Antony view next? Here's the eye of a bee. Its stinger, too. And look at these legs of lice. The intricate details he finds in such tiny creatures is astonishing.

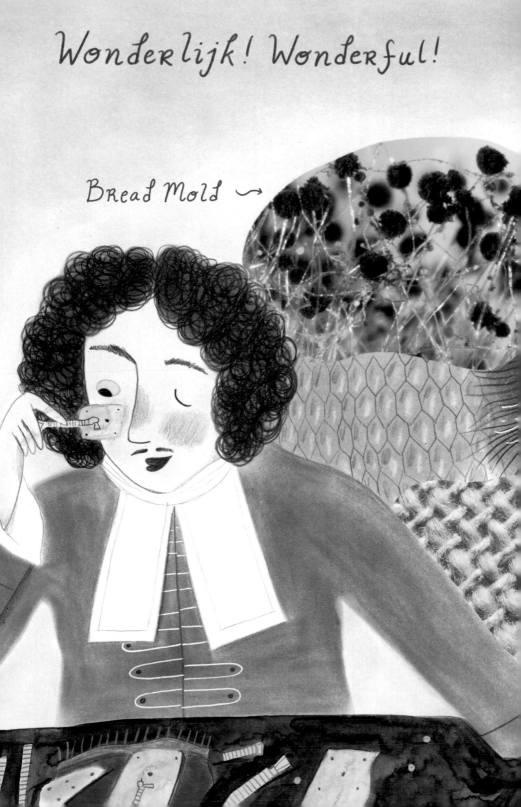

Bee Stinger

Wool

Eye of Bee

Leg of Lice

Chapter Five:
Spreading the Word

Excited by his discoveries, Antony shows some of his findings to his doctor friend Reinier de Graaf. Reinier is impressed. He encourages Antony to share his work with a group of scientists in London, called the Royal

Society. This group has the support of the English government to gather information to learn more about the natural world. It is the Royal Society who published Robert Hooke's *Micrographia*.

Antony and Reinier each write a letter to the Royal Society. Antony writes about the mold and bees and lice. Reinier writes about Antony: "I am writing to tell you that a certain most ingenious person . . . has devised microscopes which far surpass those which we have hitherto seen."

Now Antony waits for a response. And he worries. He doesn't know English or Latin, like the other scientists. He didn't go to college. Maybe his letter sounded simple and not smart enough. Maybe he angered Robert Hooke, who is a member of the Royal Society. Maybe Antony should stick to selling fabric.

As it turns out, Antony is right to worry. When the Royal Society reads his letter, they are skeptical. Who is this Antony Leeuwenhoek? Why is a draper using a microscope? Why does he write to us in Dutch? And why does his letter ramble on and on? Antony is "unlearned both in sciences and languages." But they do like that he is "exceedingly curious" about nature. After more thought, the group finds his observations of the mold and bees and lice quite informative. Antony has included new information, details Robert Hooke had missed with his microscope. They mail Antony a reply.

The letter is written in English, so Antony needs a friend to translate it to Dutch. But the news is good! The Royal Society is impressed with Antony's findings. Better yet, they want Antony to write them a letter each time he makes a discovery. They will print his work in a journal with other science articles.

Philosophical Transactions

Philosophical Transactions *is the oldest scientific journal in the world. The first issue was published by the Royal Society in 1665, and monthly issues are still printed today. Antony's first letter, and over one hundred more throughout his career, was included in this journal.*

Although Antony receives no pay for his efforts, he is filled with joy—and eager to uncover new secrets. His previous specimens, the mold and bees and lice, remain attached to their own microscopes. Those samples are glued in place, perfectly focused, and he may want to study them again later. For new work, Antony builds more microscopes. He looks at all kinds of things: coffee beans, tree rings, fly feet, snail teeth, a silkworm's spinneret (which explains where those silky threads come from!).

Antony is especially enchanted by eyes. He examines the eyes of flies, fish, birds, cats, dogs, rabbits, sheep, pigs, and cows.

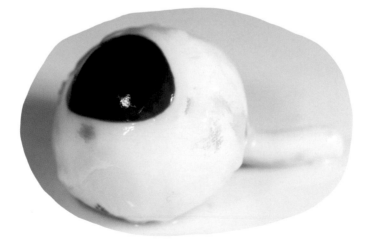

Pig eye. After it dries out, Antony will slice it with a razor and view the sections with a microscope.

He hires an artist to draw what he sees. The drawings are mailed with his letters. It is precise work, and Antony grows more skillful—and more excited—with each discovery. But his greatest discovery is yet to come.

Seeing Is Believing

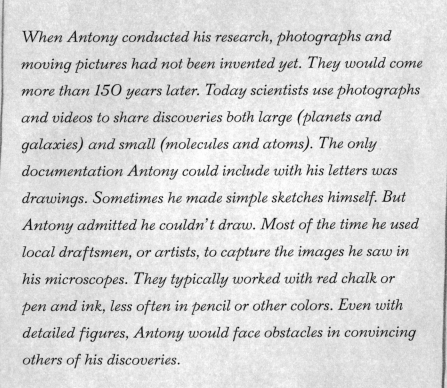

When Antony conducted his research, photographs and moving pictures had not been invented yet. They would come more than 150 years later. Today scientists use photographs and videos to share discoveries both large (planets and galaxies) and small (molecules and atoms). The only documentation Antony could include with his letters was drawings. Sometimes he made simple sketches himself. But Antony admitted he couldn't draw. Most of the time he used local draftsmen, or artists, to capture the images he saw in his microscopes. They typically worked with red chalk or pen and ink, less often in pencil or other colors. Even with detailed figures, Antony would face obstacles in convincing others of his discoveries.

Chapter Six:
Small Lake, Big Discovery

In 1674, on a warm summer day, Antony searches for samples. The water in a nearby lake looks cloudy and green. Antony is curious. He wades out near some puffy green clumps to collect a few drops of water. Back in his workshop, he builds a new microscope. Then he places the thin glass tube of lake water behind the lens. What does Antony see?

Green streaks like teeny snakes, thinner than a strand of hair. Some are coiled in spirals. Others are roundish, with a head and long tails. The streaks dart around like swimming eels, wiggling and dancing in the water. Antony can hardly believe his eyes. They are tiny creatures, moving on their own. They are alive!

Antony has never seen animals this small. No one has! Until now, people have believed that what they see with their own eyes is all that exists in the world. Could there actually be another world, invisible and hidden from human eyes?

Antony's mind whirs with questions: *What are these creatures? How did they get there? How many are there? How long do they live?* He calls them *diertgens* (in Dutch, *dier* means "animal," and *gen* means "little"). Antony wants to learn everything he can about these "little animals." So he samples water of all sorts: from rivers, canals, and the ocean; rainwater and melted snow; drinking water out of a well; even water mixed with spices such as pepper, ginger, cloves, or nutmeg.

He holds tube after tube to his eye. The water is clear. But with the microscope—full of life!

Invisible. Visible. All in a drop.

Antony cannot help but wonder at it. He finds the most creatures in pepper water—water in which he has placed whole or crushed peppercorns. He writes in his notebook, "A very pretty sight to see," after watching the little animals. He thinks and counts and measures. Antony guesses more than one million of these little animals squeezed together would equal the size of only a single grain of sand. For over a year, he continues to study the water samples. Finally, he puts his incredible discoveries into a detailed, seventeen-page letter to the Royal Society. This time, the response is much different.

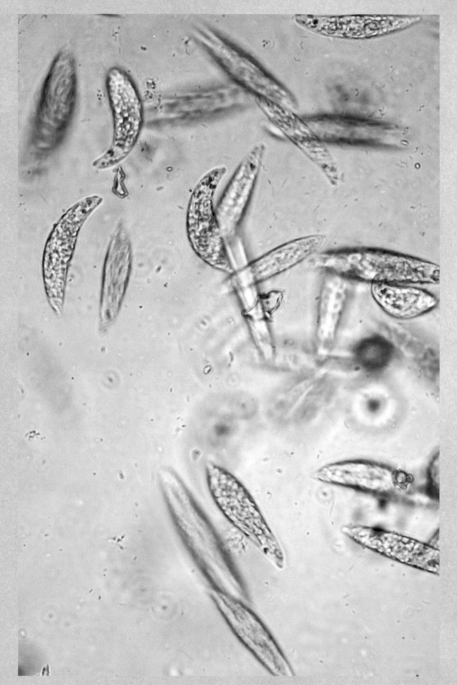

Little animals in lake water.

Chapter Seven:
A Most Important Letter

The Royal Society

The Royal Society doesn't believe Antony. They laugh.
They think the little animals are not in the water but in
Antony's imagination. If the scientists across the sea are to
believe, they need to see the animals with their own eyes.
They need to know *how* Antony found the creatures.
They need to know *how* he built his microscopes.

But Antony refuses to share his methods for
viewing. And his microscopes? He keeps their
design top-secret. Instead, Antony sends
more letters. Letters that tell of the local
townsfolk who can see his little animals.
Religious leaders, lawyers, doctors, a
medical student, and an innkeeper have
signed their names to the letters. These
eyewitnesses swear they can see the little

• *Robert Hooke* •

animals too. The Royal Society *still* doesn't believe
him. When the London scientists try with their own
microscopes, and their own water, they cannot see what
Antony sees. The Royal Society does not want to travel all
the way to Delft. Instead, they enlist Robert Hooke, the
man behind *Micrographia*, to set the record straight.

Hooke now holds the position Curator of Experiments
for the Royal Society. He spends much of his time
designing experiments and communicating with other
scientists. Although he still conducts research of his own,
it's been years since Hooke has worked with microscopes.
But he is up to the challenge! He dusts off some of his old

instruments. Antony has not provided much information on how to repeat his experiments. Hooke does know that Antony used pepper water in a thin glass tube. So he places crushed pepper into some pump water. He lets the pepper soak for two days. But when he looks through his microscope, he sees no little creatures. He tries again. This time he soaks whole peppercorns in rainwater for ten days. He uses the smallest, thinnest glass tube he can find. And he selects one of his best microscopes. Eventually, Hooke sees the little animals swimming up and down. He communicates his findings at a meeting. The scientists line up to peer through the microscope. In their meeting notes, they write, "There [is] no longer any doubt." It has been more than a year since Antony sent his long letter. Finally, the Royal Society believes.

Slowly, Antony's reputation changes. His lack of formal training is now less important. His research speaks for itself. In 1680, the London scientists make Antony a Fellow, or a member, of the Royal Society. Only the world's most respected scientists belong to the group. Antony is pleased, and he sends his gratitude by way of a letter. He promises "to strive with all my might and main, all my life long, to make myself more worthy of this honour and privilege." But he does not travel to London to sign his name on official Royal Society documents. He never attends their meetings. Antony has more important things to do.

Better than the Best

Why was Antony able to see things no one else on earth had seen? The most likely answer is the design of his microscopes. They were extremely effective because of their single-lens design. In contrast, many of Robert Hooke's microscopes were compound, which means they used several lenses stacked together. Multiple lenses increase the power of magnification. But they also increase the amount of distortion an observer sees. This distortion can affect how clear and sharp an image appears. The larger the lens, the worse the problem becomes, so Antony kept his lenses extremely small—some were no bigger than the head of a pin. They were very convex, almost spherical, for the greatest level of magnification. Of Antony's microscopes that still exist today, the most powerful magnifies an object 266 times its original size, about five to ten times more powerful than the lenses Hooke used for Micrographia.

Chapter Eight:
In the Name of Science

Despite the great honor of his being inducted into the
Royal Society, not everyone in Delft thinks Antony's
discoveries are real. Some call his work magic. Some say
Antony shows people what doesn't exist. Fortunately,
the Dutch are tolerant of different ways of thinking.
In other countries, speaking out or suggesting
ideas contrary to existing beliefs can have harsh
outcomes, including imprisonment or even death.
Many original thinkers come to the Netherlands to
write and publish books that might be censored, or
not allowed, in their own countries. Antony works
without fear. He doesn't let his neighbors' doubts
keep him from his research.

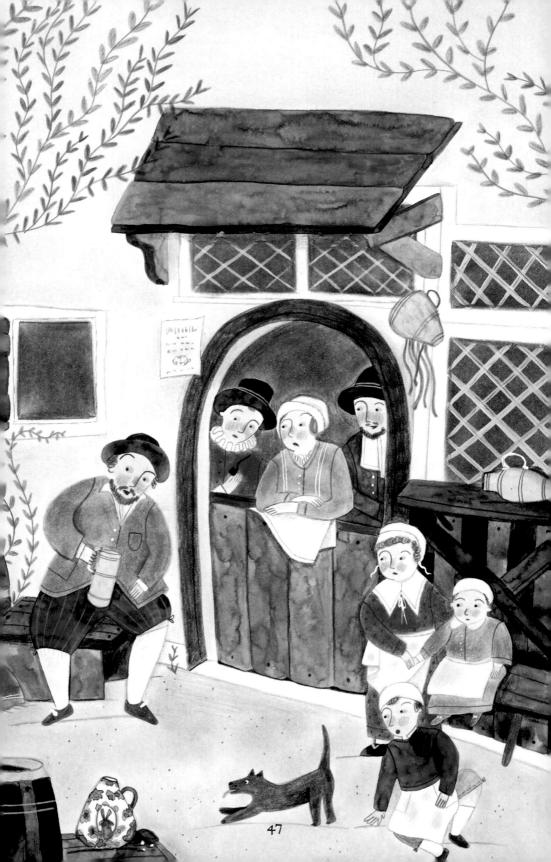

Most of Antony's research so far has been strictly observation—looking at a sample and writing down what he sees. But Antony's curiosity continues to grow. He is ready to conduct some simple experiments—tests to find answers to specific questions. And these experiments are wild, indeed!

Antony wants to know how insects are born. Do they simply appear out of mud, rotting garbage, or dead animal flesh, through *spontaneous generation,* as most people believe? Antony doesn't think so. He puts two lice into a tight black sock and wears it around the house. After six days, he finds the lice have laid ninety eggs. The white eggs are easy to count on the black sock. He leaves the sock on for ten more days to find twenty-five lice crawling on his leg, with more ready to hatch. Young insects are created from parents like themselves, he learns. They are not mysteriously formed from dirt, trash, or other nonliving things. He also learns that this experiment is itchy. Antony strips off the sock and throws it out the window. He returns to wearing his clean white socks.

Antony wants to know why the ants in his yard are carrying so much food. Do the adult ants eat it all? Antony doesn't think so. He sticks his hand down their anthill, breaking it open to look inside. He learns

48

that the food carried underground is not for the adult ants but for the larvae, or baby ants, to survive through winter. The adult ants hibernate and will not eat until spring. He also learns that the stings from ants are the worst pain he's ever felt!

At age fifty-one, Antony is proud of his healthy smile. Every day he rubs his teeth with salt, swishes with water, and wipes them with a cloth. "My teeth back and front remain as clean and white that only a few people of my age can compare with me." But in his magnifying mirror, he notices something between his back molars. He scrapes off a bit of sticky, white gunk. What could it be? When he examines the goo in a microscope, he finds lots of little animals, just like in the water. He guesses there are more little animals living in his own mouth than there are people living in the Netherlands! Antony predicts that people who clean their teeth less often will have even more little animals in their mouths. To test his hypothesis, he asks his neighbor, who has never washed his teeth in his whole life, for a sample.

"I found an unbelievably great company of living animalcules, swimming more nimbly than any I had ever seen up to this time." Antony was right. People who don't clean their teeth have the most little animals in their mouths (stinky breath, too!).

Eventually, Antony's neighbors begin to accept his oddities. They are not surprised when Antony knocks on their door to ask for a bit of earwax, a few fingernail clippings, or several strands of hair. He makes his requests in the name of science.

Word of Antony's research spreads. The draper from Delft has become one of the most famous men in the world!

What's in a Name?

The tiny creatures Antony discovered had no name because no one had seen them before. He called them diertgens, *the Dutch word for* little animal, *but when his letters were translated into English, the word was changed to* animalcules. *English scientists continued to use this term until the 1880s, when it was replaced by the French word* microbe, *originally from the Greek:* mikros *(small)* + bios *(life). Even the word* scientist *wasn't used frequently until the late 1800s. Before that, most scientists referred to themselves as* natural philosophers.

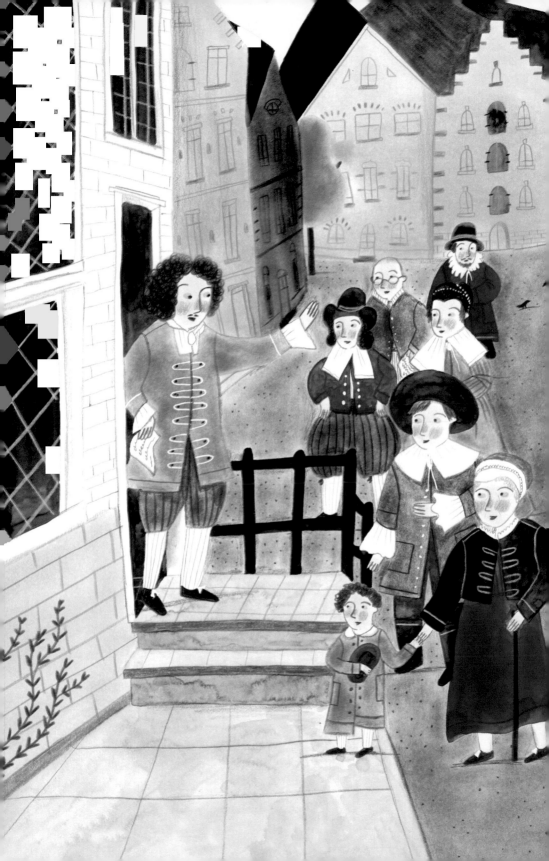

Chapter Nine:
Last Letters

Visitors travel great distances to view Antony's cabinet of curiosities: an arrangement of his microscopes, each with a sample still affixed. The guests peek through microscopes to view fish scales, flecks of gold, the insides of an oyster. It's a lucky day when Antony gives a live demonstration. Today he takes a penknife and scratches his arm several times. Into a glass tube go the skin scrapings. The visitors say this sample looks similar to the fish scales. Antony explains how the outer layer of our skin dries and peels away. A new layer of skin forms underneath.

•Peter the Great•

One of his most important visitors is Peter the Great, the tsar, or leader, of Russia. Antony presents a gift—one of his microscopes with the tail of an eel attached. The tsar is delighted when he can see blood pumping through the tail. Other visitors bring Antony gifts—strange and wonderful new samples. His favorite comes from the captain of a ship, who delivers a whale's eye preserved in a jar of brandy.

Visitors want to see the little animals, but most don't have Antony's experience or patience. Many guests complain that the microscopes give them a headache before too long. Some even say there is nothing in the water to see. Antony begins to tell his visitors that his very best microscopes are locked away. He doesn't want to waste time training those who don't take his work seriously.

Indeed, viewing hidden worlds takes patience. Most people do not want to concentrate for more than a few minutes. Antony has become a skilled scientist

because he looks at his samples for hours at a time. In some cases, he observes samples over weeks, months— even years. He repeats his observations with different microscopes and in different light, and writes down each and every detail.

Strange Samples

First to See

Although Antony didn't begin working with microscopes until he was nearly forty years old, he magnified and studied hundreds of different samples, over fifty years. He was the first person to see these specimens in such great detail. Here are some of the samples he studied:

- acids of the stomach
- alder wood
- amber
- ants
- ashwood
- bark
- beans
- beech wood
- bees

- beetles
- blood

- bones

- boxwood
- brains
- cement
- chalk
- cochineal insects
- cocoa
- coffee
- corn
- cotton
- crystalline (lens of the eye)
- ebony wood
- eels
- elm wood
- eyes
- feathers
- fir wood

- fish scales
- fleas
- flies

- frogs
- gnats
- grass
- gunpowder
- hair

- hearts
- hops grain
- kidney stones
- leaves of trees and plants

- lice

- lime tree wood
- locusts
- maggots
- magnets
- microbes

- milk
- millipedes
- mites
- mold

- moths
- muscles
- mussels
- nerves
- nettles
- nutmeg

- oak leaves

- oak wood
- oysters
- paper
- peas
- peat moss
- pepper
- periwinkle
- perspiration
- phosphorus
- plaque
- quills
- roots of trees and plants
- salt
- sand
- sap
- scorpion poison
- seeds of fruit
- shrimp
- silkworms

- skin
- snails
- spiders
- stingers (from scorpions, gnats, and nettles)
- tadpoles
- teeth
- tobacco
- tongues

- vinegar
- vomit
- weevils
- whale flesh
- wheat
- willow seeds
- willow wood
- wine
- wool

- yeast

Antony's research methods are extremely precise. He cuts his samples into paper-thin pieces using only his shaving razor. While other scientists look at the outsides of seeds, plants, and insects, Antony goes beyond the surface. He learns how hair grows, how muscles contract, how eyes focus, and how bones and teeth are formed. He pricks his own thumb with a needle to examine a sample of blood. He studies arteries, veins, and capillaries to understand how blood circulates through the body. He learns that little animals are found in water and mouths and many other places, too. Antony

watches patiently, thinks deeply, and reports carefully. He separates observable facts from old beliefs. He gains the respect of scientists. He's even awarded a medal. But Antony does not care about fame or money. He writes, "My work, which I've done for many a long year, was not pursued in order to gain the praise I now enjoy, but chiefly from a craving after knowledge, which I notice resides in me more than most other men."

He writes letters to the Royal Society until he is ninety years old. One of his last letters contains information about a pain Antony is feeling in his chest. His doctors have diagnosed him with a heart problem. But he is sure the doctors are wrong! The pain he feels is in his diaphragm, the area under his lungs. When he wheezes and coughs, a finger on his pulse tells him his heart rate is not changing. Antony does some research on the diaphragms of sheep and oxen. He writes that a blockage of blood flow to the diaphragm is the cause of the strange spasms in his chest. He is right. In time, doctors will call this condition Leeuwenhoek's disease.

Still ill, Antony continues his work with microscopes. An employee of the United East India Company, a trading company that sails from the Netherlands to places like China and India, needs to know if there is any gold in a small sample of sand he has carried from the island of Sumatra. Antony will find the answer. Even during the last days of his life, when he is confined to his bed and is

too weak to write, Antony's mind is still sharp. He asks
a friend to put some final observations down on paper.
Two days later, August 26, 1723, Antony dies.

Antony van Leeuwenhoek is the first person to see
most of what he has viewed in his microscopes over his
fifty-year career. That he was completely self-taught
makes his accomplishments all the more impressive.
Antony's work opens eyes, and minds, to hidden worlds.

Worlds we can all wonder at.

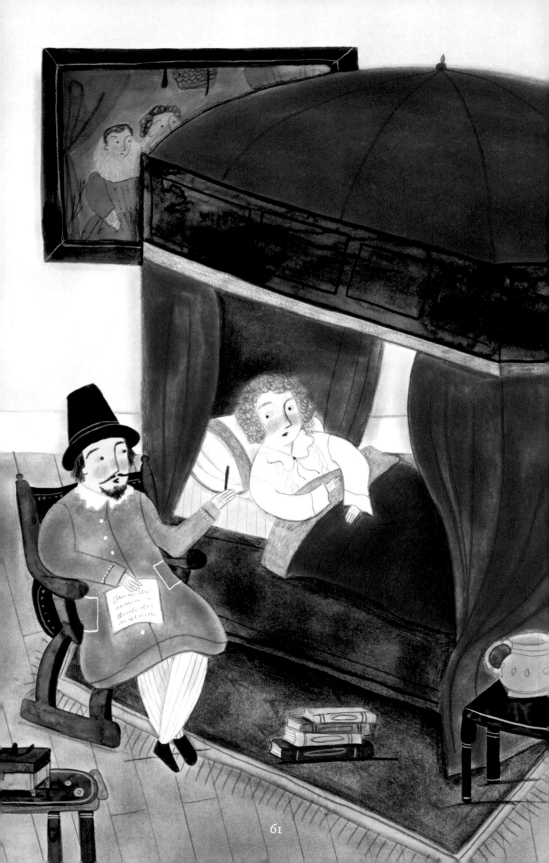

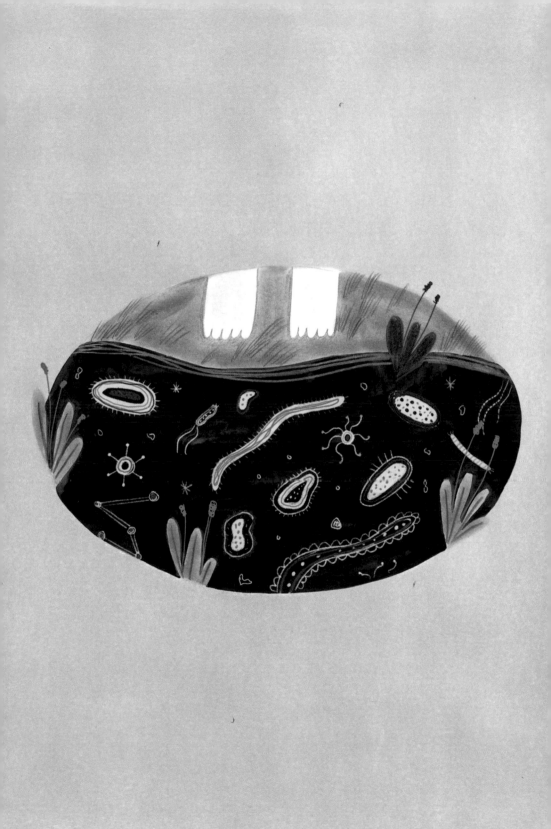

Chapter Ten:
The Father of Microbiology

With all the discoveries Antony made during his career, the possibilities of the microscope seemed endless. It's surprising to learn that Antony had little competition from other scientists in this field of study. In 1692, Robert Hooke wrote about the fate of microscopes and that they "are now reduced to almost a single Votary, which is Mr. Leeuwenhoek; besides whom, I hear of none that make any other use of that instrument, but for Diversion and Pastime." It's quite possible Antony was one of the few people using microscopes for scientific discovery in the late 1600s and early 1700s. Almost no one tried to repeat his studies for themselves. When others did take an interest in Antony's work, they were most concerned about *where* the little animals came from. They seemed less curious to find out *what* the little animals actually did. It would take one hundred years after Antony's death for scientists to return to the microscope. Their findings would eventually lead to important discoveries about illness and disease.

Antony's letters were so detailed, scientists can read them today and understand what he was viewing nearly

350 years ago. Now we know that the "little animals" were not animals at all but rather *microbes*, living things so small, they can only be seen with a microscope. There are five types of microbes: bacteria, fungi, algae, protozoa, and viruses. Antony saw four of the five types with his microscopes. Viruses are up to fifty times smaller than bacteria and too small to see with even the best simple or compound microscope.

Microbes are everywhere—from soil to oceans to Arctic snow. Microbes live on and inside humans and other animals. Most microbes are helpful. They live in our stomachs and help us digest food. They change grapes to wine and milk to yogurt. They make bread rise. They turn rotting leaves into rich soil. They help plants grow.

Some microbes can make us sick. The smallest microbes Antony studied were actually strains of bacteria, such as *Escherichia coli,* or *E. coli* for short. But in all his years of looking at microbes, Antony didn't quite make the connection between these organisms and illness. He was close! In one letter, Antony described a time when he had an upset stomach and diarrhea after eating some hot smoked beef. He examined his own feces in a microscope. Based on his letter, scientists now believe he saw a type of protozoa called *Giardia*. Most people get *Giardia* from contaminated food or water.

E. Coli and Giardia

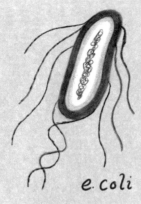

e. coli

Most strains of the E. coli bacteria are harmless to humans, but a few, such as strain O157:H7, can cause illness. This type of E. coli enters the body through contaminated food (unwashed vegetables, undercooked meat) or contaminated water (polluted streams, rivers, or lake water used to irrigate crops). The bacteria multiply in the intestines and block cells from absorbing water. This causes diarrhea and dehydration, which can be severe to fatal, especially for young children and older adults. Giardia works in a similar way in that it can cause disease in the intestines, resulting in diarrhea, stomach cramps, and vomiting. Giardia also spreads to humans through contaminated food and water.

giardia

In Antony's time, less was known about the
health benefits of personal hygiene, food safety,
and household cleanliness.

Once the connection between germs and illness was made, practices began to change, including handwashing, keeping sewage out of the water supply, and avoiding the sick.

Antony also knew that certain substances, such as vinegar or alcohol, killed his little animals. When he added vinegar to his pepper-water mixture, the microbes died. When he scraped the teeth of a man who never cleaned his mouth with water but instead rinsed with wine or brandy, he found few microbes. They had been killed by the alcohol. Antony also noted how temperature affected microbes. After drinking a cup of very hot coffee, he found no little animals on his teeth. They couldn't survive the heat.

Heat

Vinegar

During Antony's time, hundreds of thousands of people would die from illnesses such as cholera, malaria, and bubonic plague. All were caused by infections from the spread of various microbes. But it would take scientists another one hundred years to come up with the *germ theory of disease,* which states that many diseases are caused by microbes invading and reproducing in the body. Once this connection was established, many changes would be made in society. People would begin bathing more often and washing their hands. Disinfectants would be used to kill germs, especially in hospitals and operating rooms. Sick people would be kept away from the healthy. Foods and drinks would be pasteurized, or heated to a certain point, to kill harmful bacteria. Antibiotic medicines would be invented. Understanding how microbes work would eventually lead to less disease and improved public health. People could live longer and better lives.

Alcohol

Bubonic Plague

Well before scientists could see and understand microbes, there were epidemics, or times of quickly spreading disease, that wiped out entire cities and towns. One of the deadliest outbreaks took place in the mid-1300s. Bubonic plague, also known as black plague or Black Death, killed nearly 50 million people in Europe (about half of its population). The disease was spread by rats and fleas. Humans contracted the plague when they were bit by the infected fleas. But doctors didn't know this. During that time, cities were dirty and crowded, and rats and fleas were everywhere. Rats would get onto cargo ships, infecting the crew and spreading the disease from one country to another. Those who became sick usually died within days. Some people hid in their homes in an attempt to avoid the plague. Some towns were burned to the ground in an effort to slow the disease. People panicked. They thought it was the end of the world. While the worst wave of plague occurred in the 1300s, smaller outbreaks returned to different parts of the world through the 1800s. Now we know that bubonic plague is caused by a bacteria called Yersinia pestis. Very few people get bubonic plague today, and those who do are able to recover with antibiotic medicine.

Did Antony play a role in the one-hundred-year delay in understanding the link between microbes and disease? Few people were able to see and study microbes because Antony kept his lens-making techniques secret, as well as the best methods for using his delicate devices. He wouldn't sell his microscopes to other scientists. Upon his death his daughter, Maria, sent a case containing twenty-six silver microscopes to the Royal Society. Years later, after Maria's death, the rest of Antony's microscopes were auctioned off to local townspeople. Over time, the microscopes have been damaged or lost. About a dozen still exist today.

Antony always worked alone. He never wrote a book, like Robert Hooke's *Micrographia*. He didn't teach students or give lectures at universities. When asked why he didn't train others in his methods, he said, "I can't see there'd be much use." In fact, Antony seemed pleased with his secretive ways: "And I'm satisfied too that not one man in a thousand is capable of such study, because it needs much time . . . and you must always keep on thinking about these things, if you are to get any results. And over and above all, most men are not curious to know: nay, some even make no bones about saying, What does it matter whether we know this or not?"

On the other hand, it's possible that Antony's lack of education gave him an advantage. He had no teachers to

tell him how to think or what to believe. Maybe feeling like an outsider gave Antony the motivation to work hard and come up with new theories of his own. Still, he wasn't afraid to change his mind about something, if new facts surfaced. "I will only say once more that 'tis my habit to hold fast to my notions only until I'm better informed, or till my observations make me go over to others: and I'll never be ashamed thus to chop and change."

Either way, the work Antony did with microscopes forever changed the way we see the world around us. Antony's letters set a strong foundation for future scientists to build upon. Now we know that the majority of living things on earth are invisible to our eyes. Today Antony van Leeuwenhoek is known as "the Father of Microbiology," the study of organisms too small to see without a microscope.

Over time, Antony's microscopes have been damaged or lost. About a dozen still exist today.

Author's Note

Antony was born nearly four hundred years ago. He was about forty years old when he started working with microscopes. And for the next fifty years, everything Antony saw through his microscopes, he was the first person to see it. Although he didn't invent the microscope, he was the first to use it so extensively. Over the course of his life, he wrote more than two hundred letters to the Royal Society. They read more like casual conversations with friends than formal reports of data. In my favorite of Antony's letters, he sat by a fire and used his right hand to drink a cup of hot tea. He put his left hand into a clear glass jar. When the warmth of the fire and tea made his hand sweat, he collected the drops in the jar to study with his microscopes. He loved to use himself as a research guinea pig! Antony was curious about so many fields of study: insects (entomology), plants (botany), animals (zoology), tissue (histology), blood (hematology), and microscopic life (microbiology). Today scientists usually focus on only one area of study.

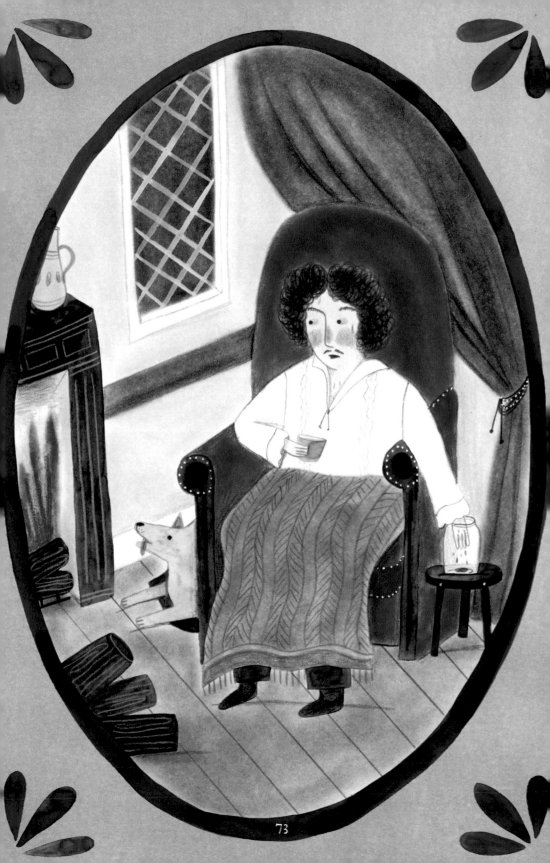

Even with the awards and visits from famous people, Antony could lack confidence. In 1699, he wrote a letter to a scholar in Italy, sharing experiments he made with insects in canal water. The creatures produced eggs, which hatched more tiny insects, helping Antony make a case against the widespread theory of spontaneous generation. But Antony ended the letter with "You will excuse, illustrious Signor, my boldness, in taking up

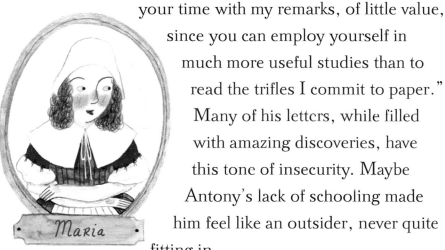

Maria

your time with my remarks, of little value, since you can employ yourself in much more useful studies than to read the trifles I commit to paper." Many of his letters, while filled with amazing discoveries, have this tone of insecurity. Maybe Antony's lack of schooling made him feel like an outsider, never quite fitting in.

Antony was married twice. He and his first wife, Barbara, had five children. Unfortunately, only his daughter, Maria, survived through infancy. Antony was not paid for his research or his publications in the science journals. He held other jobs, besides his work as a draper (maybe the additional income helped Antony purchase the materials he needed for making microscopes). One such job was in a courtroom in the town hall, where Antony did office tasks for some of

the city lawyers and judges. He also worked as a land surveyor and a wine gauger. All of these jobs required measurement and attention to detail. But none of them made the lasting impact on the world that his lifelong research with microscopes did.

Historians don't agree on the date Antony first began making microscopes. Some say he had the means to begin around 1659 and that he'd already built microscopes before his visit to London. They believe he brought one on his trip and used it to examine the chalk cliffs sample. Other researchers believe it wasn't until Antony saw the book *Micrographia* that his interest in microscopes grew. They say it's no coincidence that the first samples Antony wrote about were the same specimens Robert Hooke included in that book. In 1673, in his second letter to the Royal Society, Antony wrote that his microscopes were "newly invented." Historians do agree that Antony built more than five hundred microscopes

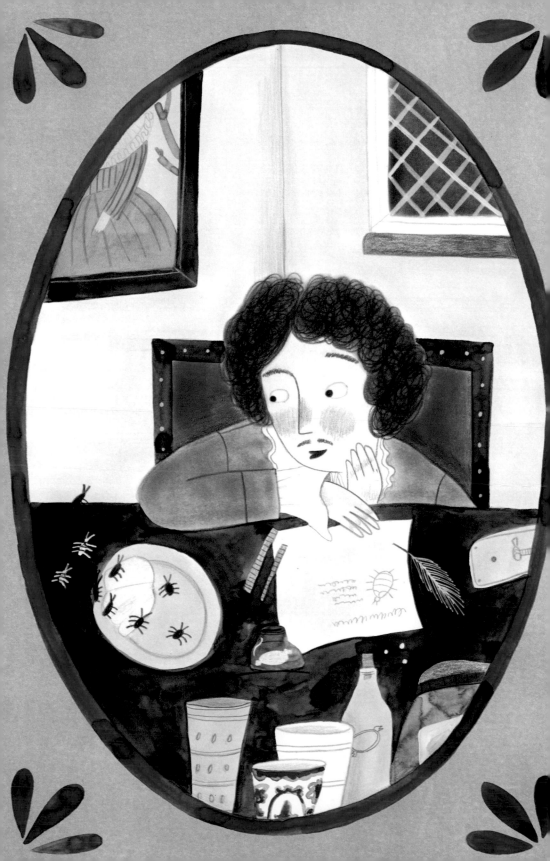

during his career. He often fixed his samples to the instruments with glue or wax. Instead of looking at multiple samples with the same microscope, he built new microscopes for new specimens. He did this partly because the devices were composed of softer metals, like copper or silver, and the threads of the positioning screws would change over time, making it difficult to maintain focus. Different lens strengths worked better for different samples, so they were matched accordingly. Sadly, most of these instruments have been lost, damaged, or discarded as junk when their new owners couldn't figure out how to use them properly. The few that exist today can be found in various museums in the Netherlands, Germany, and Belgium.

In the end, what stands out the most may be Antony's curiosity and passion for learning. "I have spent a lot more time than many people would believe," Antony wrote about his observations, "yet I made them with pleasure."

Timeline of Events

World events listed in red.

1632 Antony Leeuwenhoek is born on October 24 in Delft, Netherlands, to Philips Thonisz and Margriete Jacobs.

1638 Antony's father dies. His mother is left to raise five children.

1640 Antony's mother marries painter Jacob Molijn. Jacob has five children from previous marriages.

1641 Eight-year-old Antony is sent to live and study at a boarding school in Warmond, about fifteen miles from his home.

1644 René Descartes's *Principles of Philosophy* is published in Amsterdam. The book presents a method for thinking scientifically about the natural world.

1646 Antony lives with his lawyer uncle in Benthuizen.

1648 At sixteen, Antony works as draper's apprentice for linen merchant William Davidson in Amsterdam.

1654 Antony marries Barbara de Meij.

1655 Antony buys a house in Delft and sets up his shop. This is where he will live and work for the rest of his life.

1656 Antony's daughter, Maria, is born. His four other children will not survive infancy.

1660 The Royal Society is founded in London in order to gain knowledge about the natural world.

1660 Antony takes a second job as a chamberlain, or office manager, of a courtroom in Delft.

1664 An outbreak of bubonic plague kills more than 10 percent of Amsterdam's population. Areas of England, Italy, and Spain are affected as well. Doctors do not know the cause and recommend only rest and a healthy diet.

1665 Robert Hooke's book *Micrographia* is published. In the book, Hooke coins the term *cell* from his observation of a thin slice of cork through a microscope. The boxlike structures remind him of the small rooms or "cells" where monks live.

1665 Delft artist Johannes Vermeer paints *Girl with a Pearl Earring.* Vermeer may have used special lenses to help him paint realistic portraits.

1666 Antony's wife, Barbara, dies.

1668 Antony travels to London and likely sees Hooke's *Micrographia.*

1669 Antony is certified as a land surveyor, measuring and recording the size, shape, and terrain of plots of land for sale.

1671 Antony marries Cornelia Swalmius.

1673 Antony writes his first letter to Henry Oldenburg, secretary of the Royal Society, detailing his findings with mold, bees, and lice.

1673 At age forty, Antony sees his first letter published in the scientific journal *Philosophical Transactions*.

1674 Antony observes red blood cells in blood taken from his own hand.

1674 Antony observes "little animals" (microbes) in water taken from Berkelse Mere, a lake near Delft.

1676 Antony observes bacteria.

1676 Antony writes a seventeen-page letter to the Royal Society detailing his observations of microbes in various types of water.

1677 Eight Delft citizens write letters to the Royal Society attesting to living creatures in Antony's water samples.

1677 In November, Robert Hooke is finally able to replicate Antony's findings. The Royal Society can now see the microbes for themselves.

1679 Antony is appointed as a wine gauger, inspecting the city's imported and exported wines.

1680 Antony is elected a Fellow by the Royal Society. The honor encourages him to continue with his research.

1685 Antony adds *van* to his name; he signs his letters *Antony van Leeuwenhoek* for the rest of his career.

1694 Antony's wife Cornelia dies.

1698 Peter the Great visits Antony and is impressed by his microscopes.

1723 On his deathbed, Antony requests that his two final letters, one detailing the reason for his own illness, be translated into Latin.

1723 Antony dies on August 26, at the age of ninety, in his home in Delft, Netherlands.

1723 Antony's daughter, Maria, sends a cabinet containing twenty-six microscopes to the Royal Society.

1747 After Maria's death, Antony's cabinet of curiosities, including 531 microscopes and lenses, is auctioned off to local buyers.

1847 Carl Zeiss, a German lens maker, begins selling compound microscopes with improved resolution. Principles of optics are better understood, and problems with lighting and chromatic aberration, a distortion that affects the sharpness and color of a sample, have been solved.

1860 Louis Pasteur, a French chemist, develops germ theory, which identifies germs as the cause of disease. He invents pasteurization, using heat to kill harmful bacteria contained in wine, milk, and beer.

1867 Joseph Lister, a British surgeon, builds on Pasteur's germ theory in the operating room. He uses antiseptic solutions to protect the wounds of surgery patients. Death from infection begins to decline.

1870 Robert Koch, a German physician, studies microbes and their link to infectious disease, leading to a better understanding of anthrax, cholera, and tuberculosis.

1931 The first electron microscope is invented. It uses a beam of electrons, instead of rays of light, to examine the smallest objects, such as viruses and molecules. Because the wavelength of electrons is shorter than the wavelength of light, electron microscopes are able to view objects one thousand times smaller than a microscope with lenses.

1950 The first superbugs, strains of bacteria that are resistant to, or can no longer be killed by, antibiotic medicine, are discovered. Superbugs are able to adapt to the drugs meant to kill them and change their structure in order to survive.

Today Electron microscopes can magnify an object more than 2 million times its original size, about 7,500 times more powerful than Antony's best single-lens design existing today.

Salt and pepper magnified with electron microscope.

Antony's cabinet of curiosities held specimens from a variety of plants and animals. He used his own china teacups to store many of his water samples.

Glossary

algae—small, single-celled or multicellular plantlike organisms with no leaves, stems, or roots. Algae grow in water and damp places

antibiotic—a medicine that stops the growth of or destroys microbes, used in the treatment of diseases

apprentice—a person who learns a trade from another skilled person, ususally with no pay other than food and shelter

apothecary—a store where medicines and drugs are sold

bacteria—tiny living organisms found almost everywhere on earth, from soil to oceans to Arctic snow. Bacteria live on and inside humans and other animals. Although some cause harm, most kinds of bacteria are helpful.

cabinet of curiosities—a collection of odd or extraordinary objects, grouped into categories, like today's museums

cell—the basic unit of any living organism. Most cells can only be seen with a microscope

concave—curving inward, like a bowl; a **concave lens** spreads light rays, as in a flashlight.

convex—bulging outward, like a bean; a **convex lens** focuses light rays, as in a magnifying glass.

draper—a person who sells fabrics and other supplies for dressmaking and sewing

epidemic—a spread of infectious disease affecting many people in a community at one time

fungus—a small, single-celled or multicellular organism that reproduces by sending out tiny spores. Some examples are yeast, mold, and mushrooms. Plural: **fungi.**

germ theory—the idea that many diseases are caused by microbes in the body

larva—a very young, wormlike form or stage of an insect. Plural: **larvae.**

lens—a clear piece of glass or plastic, usually curved, that spreads or focuses light rays. A lens can be concave or convex.

louse—a small insect that lives on the skin of people, animals, and birds. Plural: **lice.**

magnifying glass—another name for a convex lens, a lens that makes an object appear larger than it really is

merchant—a person who buys or sells goods to earn

money; a shopkeeper or tradesperson

microbe—a living thing so small, it can only be seen with a microscope

Micrographia—an illustrated book by Robert Hooke containing observations he made through different lenses. Published in 1665, it became a bestseller and inspired many people to become interested in microscopes.

microscope—an instrument that uses lenses to make objects look larger than they actually are. A **simple microscope** contains one lens. A **compound microscope** contains more than one lens.

organism—an individual animal, plant, or single-celled lifeform; a living thing

plaque—a sticky, white film, made from bits of food, saliva, and bacteria, that grows on teeth

protozoan—a small, single-celled organism that can move around and eat food. Plural: **protozoa.**

spherical—having the shape of a sphere; round or globe-shaped

spontaneous generation—the idea that living organisms can be made from nonliving matter

thread count—in fabric, the number of vertical and horizontal threads per square inch. The higher the thread count, the better the quality.

Antony's figures of bacteria found in the human mouth from his letter written in 1683.

Source Notes

Unless otherwise noted, direct quotes were taken from original letters translated by Clifford Dobell in *Antony van Leeuwenhoek and His "Little Animals,"* first published in 1932.

Introduction
"At such perfection in this tiny creature I did greatly marvel": p. 147.

5. Spreading the Word
"I am writing to tell you": pp. 40–41.

"unlearned both in sciences and languages": p. 43.

"exceedingly curious": p. 43.

6. Small Lake, Big Discovery
"What" are these creatures?: p. 117.

"A very pretty sight to see": p. 137.

7. A Most Important Letter
"there [is] no longer any doubt": p. 186.

"to strive with all my might": p. 50.

8. In the Name of Science

"My teeth back and front remain as clean": Schierbeek,
   Measuring the Invisible World, p. 72.

*"I found an unbelievably great company of living
   animalcules"*: p. 241.

9. Last Letters

"My work, which I've done for many a long year":
   pp. 82–83.

10. The Father of Microbiology

"are now reduced to almost a single Votary": p. 52.

"I can't see there'd be much use": p. 325.

"And I'm satisfied too that not one man in a thousand":
   p. 325.

"I will only say once more that 'tis my habit": p. 73.

Author's Note

"You will excuse, illustrious Signor, my boldness": Hoole,
   Select Works of Antony van Leeuwenhoek, p. 89.

"newly invented": p. 42.

"I have spent a lot more time than many people": p. 74.

Selected Bibliography

Books

Dobell, Clifford. *Antony van Leeuwenhoek and His "Little Animals."* 1932. Reprint, New York: Dover Publications, 1960.

Hooke, Robert. *Micrographia; or, Some Physiological Descriptions of Minute Bodies Made by Magnifying Glasses, with Observations and Inquiries Thereupon.* London: Royal Society, 1665.

Hoole, Samuel, trans. *The Select Works of Antony van Leeuwenhoek, Containing His Microscopical Discoveries in Many of the Works of Nature,* vol. 2. 1807. Reprint, San Bernardino, CA: BiblioLife, 2016.

Roberts, Benjamin. *Through the Keyhole: Dutch Child-Rearing Practices in the 17th and 18th Century: Three Urban Elite Families.* Hilversum, Netherlands: Verloren, 1998.

Schierbeek, Abraham. *Measuring the Invisible World: The Life and Works of Antoni van Leeuwenhoek.* London and New York: Abelard-Schuman, 1959.

Snyder, Laura J. *Eye of the Beholder: Johannes Vermeer, Antony van Leeuwenhoek, and the Reinvention of Seeing.* New York: W. W. Norton, 2015.

Websites

Alle de Brieven, a collection of Leeuwenhoek's letters, translated into English by the Digital Library for Dutch Literature. (www.dbnl.org/tekst/leeu027alle00_01; accessed February 10, 2017)

Brian J. Ford Website. "The Leeuwenhoek Legacy." (www.brianjford.com/wlegacya.htm; accessed April 12, 2016)

Lens on Leeuwenhoek. (lensonleeuwenhoek.net; accessed March 24, 2016)

The Royal Society. (www.royalsociety.org: accessed May 6, 2016)

For Young Readers

Bolt, Marvin. "Making Microscope Lenses in the 1600s." Corning Museum of Glass. September 22, 2016. (blog. cmog.org/2016/09/22/making-microscope-lenses-in-the-1600s)

Davies, Nicola. *Tiny Creatures: The World of Microbes.* Somerville, MA: Candlewick Press, 2014.

Lichtman, Flora, and Sharon Shattuck. "Animated Life: Seeing the Invisible." *New York Times.* September 16, 2014. (vimeo.com/106297648)

Index

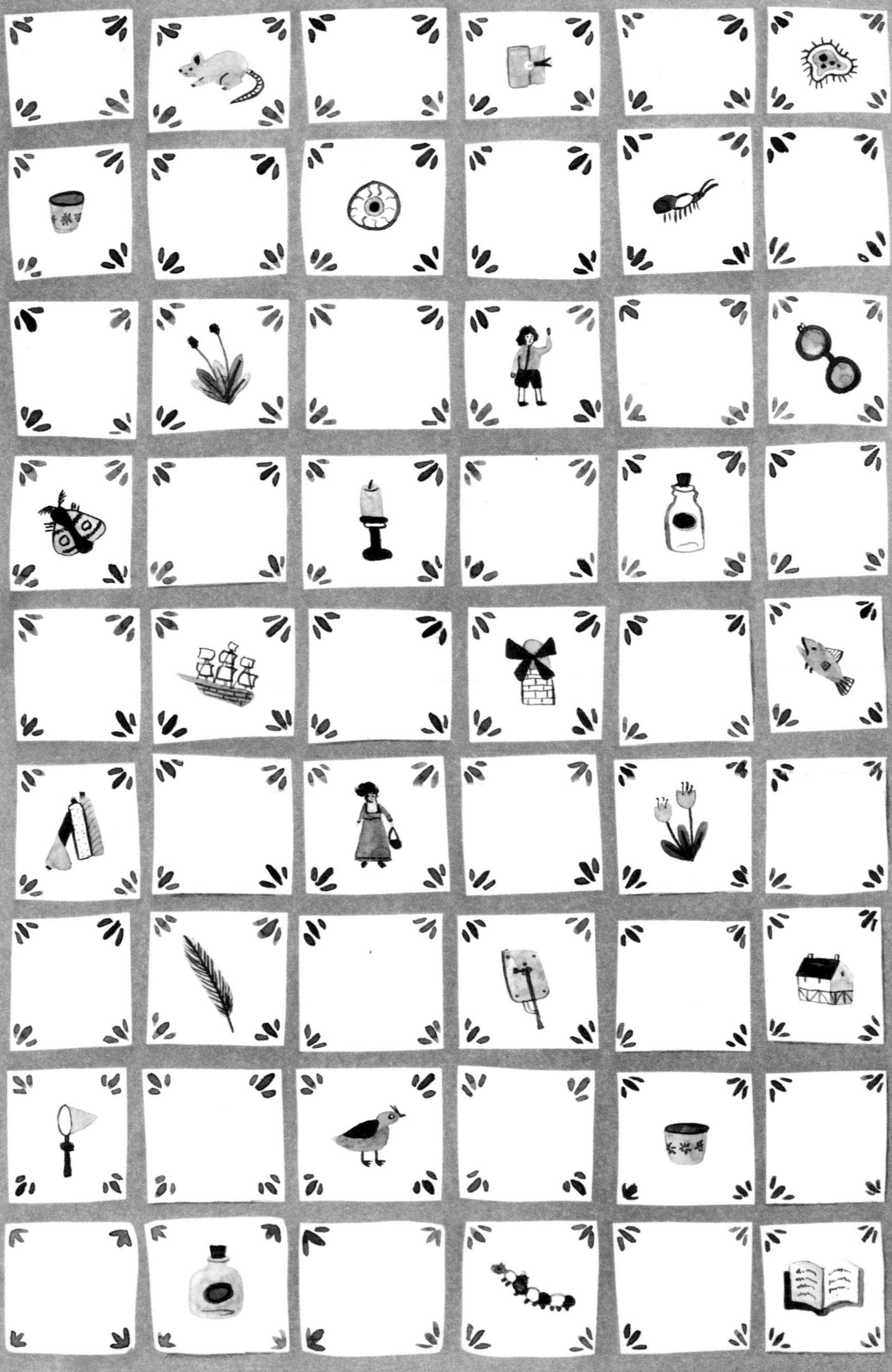